HOW TO

NOT BE

AFRAID OF

EVERYTHING

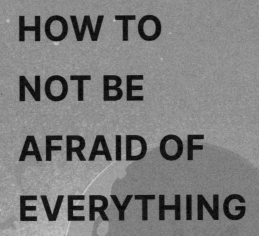

HOW TO NOT BE AFRAID OF EVERYTHING

Jane Wong

Alice James Books
Farmington, Maine
alicejamesbooks.org

10 9 8 7 6 5 4 3 2

Alice James Books are published by Alice James Poetry Cooperative, Inc., an affiliate of the
University of Maine at Farmington.

Alice James Books
114 Prescott Street
Farmington, ME 04938
www.alicejamesbooks.org

Library of Congress Cataloging-in-Publication Data

Names: Wong, Jane, author.
Title: How to not be afraid of everything / Jane Wong.
Description: Farmington, ME : Alice James Books, [2022]
Identifiers: LCCN 2021010187 (print) | LCCN 2021010188 (ebook) | ISBN
   9781948579216 (paperback) | ISBN 9781948579452 (epub)
Subjects: LCGFT: Poetry.
Classification: LCC PS3623.O59775 H69 2022 (print) | LCC PS3623.O59775
   (ebook) | DDC 811/.6--dc23
LC record available at https://lccn.loc.gov/2021010187
LC ebook record available at https://lccn.loc.gov/2021010188

Alice James Books gratefully acknowledges support from individual donors, private foundations,
the University of Maine at Farmington, the National Endowment for the Arts, the Amazon Literary
Partnership, and the Maine Arts Commission, an independent state agency supported by the
National Endowment for the Arts.

Cover art: Illustration created by Kimothy Wu (@kimothywuart)

CONTENTS

For my grandparents
and those lost during the Great Leap Forward

i will keep the door unlocked
until something human comes.

—Lucille Clifton

MAD

Jane, deceived by _____ time and again, should not _____ but she _____ and slept with curled fists.

The rat catching a ride on the turtle wins _____. Ugly and coarse, but _____.

Beware of strangers who _____ and win your _____ and lick the sweat off your nose in false _____, just to taste their own _____.

Do not trust in owls, in heads that spin. Heads should not spin nor stink, like ammonia in the armpits, like a habit of _____.

Do not pause to watch insects _____ like dangling lights. Their soft speckled bodies, a minutia of buzzing dandelion seeds, have already _____ you in the neck. Blood on their spindle tongues. This is a metaphor for _____.

There are no wolves in this tale. Only handsome _____ with pea-green eyes who will tell you: "You are as soft as _____." Then, they will carefully cut _____ and _____.

Seek only the smallest kindness, of shaking out a pebble from a neighbor's shoe, to do unto others what you _____. Did you swallow _____?

Jane, called "intense." Surely, heads spun, owl-struck, stating: "If only she _____." Called "feisty," "talks too _____ or talks too _____." Often: "Too smart for _____ good," "I never thought you'd be _____, looking like _____," "you have big eyes for a _____," "curiously strong" or "_____weak," or "it's just _____ and it's for the best."

Her hair though, is the best, and is remarkably like kindling and okay for _____ to touch, light, and ingest in flame, strand by _____. Ignore when she says _____ or _____. This is _____ of Jane.

Jane rubbed salt all over her body to become a dissolving _____ and thusly, rightfully so, _____ right out of this _____ world.

EVERYTHING

I am the type to go to bed with my feet dirty

A man calling from a balcony is not to be trusted

In 1988, the nation sings a song I can't understand but I sing it because everyone looks at me like a thief and no one likes a thief

Algae gathers in plastic cups along the Jersey Shore

The dull prongs of a fork still count as a weapon

I gather plastic cups along the shore and shake them out to use for tea, juice, a home for my toothbrush

The Pledge of Allegiance is a building ledge, an alleged crime, a leg crossed over another leg, a plea gone askew, a glance shared in a room with someone else who looks like you

Hundreds of toxic wild boars are roaming across northern Japan and it would be a mistake to identify with them

In 1960, my grandmother holds no knife in no tall wheat

When washing her feet, my grandmother tells me she spent decades without shoes, wonders if the mud misses her

I am a good daughter and I can repeat this indefinitely without taking a breath

Often, I call out to myself just to hear an echo, to hear something moving in the walls like a healthy family of rats

My mother has been told, repeatedly: "You can't walk here"

Here is a white stone, a white fence, a white sea gull, a white jug of milk, a white candle, a white duvet, a white patio, a white bar of soap to wash your mouth out

Sometimes I dream in Cantonese and I have no idea what is being said

You grow to love what you create, pouring out of your mouth

In 1988, my father sees his reflection in the rearview mirror and identifies with the blood moon lighting his way to Atlantic City

From a balcony, a man yells at me: "You need some white dick" and I turn into a boar

我在广东做梦

My father disappears for weeks and my mother keeps weeding the garden, pulling cigarettes from the splintering tomatoes I will devour

I study asymptotes for months and dream in curves—almost but never touching

My mother writes in her English diary for night school: "I hate him I hate him I hate him I hate him I" and her ESL teacher only gives her a check, so I give her a check plus

To be a good daughter means to carry everything with you at all times, the luggage of the past lifted to the mouth

When we look at each other, my mother laughs like an overripe tomato on a windowsill

In 1989, I spent months assembling a puzzle map of the United States of America and the teacher said, "Good job, Jane" and then louder and slower like a drowning sloth: "Gooooood Jahhhhhhb, Jane" and I did not touch a single piece

Bloody drunk and a blood moon, my father fights with another gambler and jabs at his arm with a dull fork and they both laugh celestially

你是一只美丽的野猪

During elementary school, I did not say a single word, not even when called on, and thus the teachers and administrators decided I could not speak English because they looked at me

Mao Zedong explains math: "In geometry, I just drew a picture of an egg—that was enough geometry for me"

My grandfather was jailed by the Red Army sometime between 1966 and 1976 and my mother says: "I saw him cry when I tried to visit. He wanted to eat the bao I made for him"

Algae gathers, gleaming like a jewel, on the head of my 5th-grade betta fish

Counterrevolutionaries during the Cultural Revolution are likened to "finding a bone inside an egg"

I was born, healthy, in the year of the rat

The man on the balcony invests in a foldable set of two chairs and one table in egg-shell-white—mold resistant, perfect for outdoor use

你不敢看我

I was ten when I willed a rock to fall off a ledge, just by staring at it long enough

AN ALTAR

A glass of water half   full with my lipstick   along the edge

to keep you afloat   to let you know I   kissed it first

THE FRONTIER

The frontier arranges itself
around me like a moat.
The frontier drops fruit
upon my head. I break open,
hot cantaloupe in winter.
I wobble around, spilling fruit
everywhere. All day, fruit flies
pay their respects. Dear beloved
country, dear beloved superfunds
and farm turbines in corn-
ruin. Go sweetly into the light:
fluorescent and pinker than
any tongue I could pray to have.
And can't I have what I've been
promised? This shore and this sea,
shining always, thereafter?

I asked for too much.
That was the problem.
In a sky lit with smoke,
my mother peels shrimp and
I carry the shells into the yard
and bury them. What we plant
will grow twofold, or so we've
been told. Frontier, shed thy
grace on thee! Grace descends
like locust. Onion grass sprouts
alongside my father's beard—
all awry. The frontier mills about
in the yard without a rake or
shovel or hand to give out.
The frontier warns me:
an eye for an eye as far as
the eye can see. And what is there
to see? Fields upon fields of
frost, of rusty shipping containers,
of highway rest stops my grandmother

steals napkins from. *Is it worth it?*
I ask her. *To live in this place where*
you fill your pockets with stones?
My grandmother opens her eyes
in the middle of the night:
What you have not noticed
asks you to look again.

A new car arrives and my mother
beams with the pride of
a glowworm. She's spun to
the nines: gold drips from her ears
like wax. Even the flies along
the windowsill turn to gold.
It's hard to breathe in this
luxurious air. I walk around
the house with a mask.
There's construction in the garage,
construction in the kitchen.
Every immigrant has that one
drawer full of plastic bags in
plastic bags. We open them
when we knock a wall down.
Tessellations of the frontier:
bags floating off in Great Northern
air. Go forth—my *thank-yous,*
my pocked plastic cheeks,
my lunch money
hunkering down in clouds.

Ruin gives back whether
you want such charity or not.
In this country, hurricanes have
the name of any decent receptionist.
Sandy, my mother says, hacking
at fallen branches with her cleaver.
Sandy, your refinery in our throats
and eyes—diamonds and dimes.
In Jersey, to exit the front

door, you better be a customer.
Even the moths leave through the alley,
wings slick with griddle grease.
In the alley, my brother and I jump
on mountains of cardboard and
packing peanuts. I swallowed
a packing peanut once and plastic
leaked from my eyes. *Sandy,*
wipe away your tears! My mother
braces her back against
the ribs of a hallway arch.

TENANTS

Above: my neighbor's feet, fussing   from room to room,
    velvet hooves   tendering my head. Was the fruitcake

curdling? Would the mail make it there on time (it must
    make it there on time)? Below: I try to light

the stove. Little clicks of the tongue, heat and water,   my altar.
    Underground: my grandfather breathes through a silk jacket,

a dandelion mane resting between   his lips. Here: every living
    thing is an altar. Sweet worms kiss   his knuckles to sleep,

loose doorknobs I open: story after story. My family:
    a spiral staircase, a fish spine   picked clean, the snail's

miasmic song. 1982: sun gasping through splintering snow,
    a lemon slice folded   in my mother's cup, a generous

bulb, a lighthouse across oceans she can not see. 1985: we slept in
    a split-level attic,   squirrels running across

the beams. 1964: my grandfather offers my mother one egg.
    Her brother looks on, fists   full of ash. 1967: to make

the body dance with sticks and stones to break   alone. Within:
    prison, rose finch feathers float through bars, what he can not

talk about. My grandfather sings to me in a ladybug-speckled coffin,
    the color of good teeth.   Above: my grandmother keeps

heaps upon heaps of oil containers, poured   and repurposed
    in hunched Fanta plastic. This living can be so quiet sometimes,

you can hear the lights   humming. Moss slinks into my walls
    and is painted over, white   to mint. I touch

the wall, these porous lives, this dense   understory. Today: I cut
    a telescope   in two to see everything inside, out:
                            new.

WHAT I TELL MYSELF BEFORE I SLEEP

Step into the consequences — de-robe in remainders of what sweet division — keep a housefly as a watchman — let him flick his legs with signs of misfortune —let him tousle his nose-like hairs at the pale grass smell of men — disaster: after all — you are the type of person to watch someone nap — make no mistake, that *is* the gentle curve of the moon — not the bridge of a nose you've kissed — showing itself in broad daylight — cratered in hope and — vulgarity, how you embarrass everyone in this grocery store — holding lettuce the way you do — to love the one who does not — does not — divide — what wreck, the watchman says, licking his compound eye — how dare you — become the old dog growing weak at the ankles — grease in the ear fur — watch your mother place mangoes — to ripen along the windowsill — feel the very green of your self — fibers in the teeth, running along the pit — look into a telescope — there: nothing but someone else's fear — old batteries in a drawer with exploded pens — there, there: maybe you've been too careful with the words you use — searched too closely for signs — a roll of paper towels left out in the rain — a picnic table, legs sinking in otherworldly mud —remainders: tired of having to see the big picture, glaucomic at the edges — must we crawl across the floor — just to see the world from another angle

A COSMOLOGY

I told the earth to settle back
     down, to lay deep in its mud
armchair, to soften the static

flaring from its mouth.
     Can we slow down, tender
those we miss? The sky—

ledge or loom—dangles in my
     grandfather's mouth, jaw-
bone in the burial ground.

In my dream last night,
     he was a golden beet in
January snow. I grate

ginger over an ant hole,
     certain it would gild them
too. I repeat: I will not be afraid

that the world is about power.
     My ghosts fill me with feathers,
my lungs: a mane unplucked.

The near promise of erasure
     settles me in this world, buzzing
fridge fluorescence. The rotting

head of broccoli in my grandmother's
     bowl blooms with power.
What we keep, we eat, what we

love, we break off. In another world,
     a bee falls headfirst into
a pitcher of rice wine. I set

an altar, the altar billows
     with ferns good in any soup.

Ants sing along the stems.

I scrub the sugar off my face
    and offer this kiss:
my gold-leaf self, sheet by sheet.

THE FRONTIER

What ends in this country
simply does not. Onward
and onward and so forth.
Thus declared. In the half-light
of a mosquito's bite, we keep
moving. Each mountain
rinses the sky of its crimes.
My father empties his pockets,
stunned and stalled in Atlantic
wreck. No business, no job, no two-
for-one peaches. The frontier
consoles me: this land of
opportunity, leaden, stolen,
all for a lump sum. I slump
over the proving ground.
Credentials gilded, framed
in hovering horseflies.
Each day, I translate
documents and bills and
government forms for my family.
My grandfather sings his songbird
to sleep. Jersey unsmogs itself
in a dream. What creeps
into these stars: a sun spool,
a lullaby for unsung shores,
my grandfather's brown mole
on his right cheek, expansive
as prairie. Plumped as a California
raisin in tears. Proof.
A signature here and there,
in flourishing perpetuity.

On another continent, seaweed blooms.
Bouquets of green stuffed
in the mouth, salt and wind,
and my father's desire to see
the other side. What did they tell you

to do? In case of emergency.
Misunderstanding or worse. To puff up
your chest to intimidate? Puffer fish?
Or play dead, a sleeping lizard?
Or gamble and sulk and slink
away, as the frontier thusly
declared?

Your rights, do you know?
To not let in. To speak
to whom? To sign over
nothing? Silence as a remainder:
how I failed at long division,
wrapping my arms around
each wrong digit. My brother
and I hid under tables
when someone knocked
on the door. Strangers: another
kind of earthquake. Between
overtime night shifts, my mother
paces. She tries a new path, orbits
our neighborhood to ease her
vertigo. A marvel, how we set foot
on the moon. A marvel, shift after
shift, how she is even moving,
awake. Strangers: a neighbor
yells at my mother from behind
her screen door, a partition for
mosquitoes, flies, liability.
She tells my mother: *You can't
walk here.* My mother is all breath
and moon smoke through
grit and grids:
I live here too.
To love a country that refuses
to look you in the eye.
To love what keeps moving
even when it shouldn't.
We build our houses, homes.
We pull splinters from our knees,

one after the other, bending
each time, as if in prayer.

Our rights, inalienable
or alien always? The fearful
and fearless in pink morning light:
semitrucks rushing onto
on-ramps. The overlapping layers
of highway turning as I turn
in my sleep, right and left, right
and right, like pancakes flipping
in the diner of my dreams, safe
from doors, neither knocked on,
nor screened. But when I wake,
I am shaking in my own
snot. Who? Who has been
consoling me again?

Remainders of silence:
my mother's refusal to hide,
to be told what to do or
not to do. The frontier bows
before us, in apology or majesty
ingested. *Break bread, eat
instead*. Containers of oil and fat,
filled and refilled again. Russet
potato cheeks, Red Lobster birthdays,
buttered rolls fitted in purses,
puckered for a kiss. What is possible:
letting bread go stale. Bread itself:
possible. Seeded, unseeded,
rosemarried, whatever and whatnot,
the frontier is winning. Hard to undo
this want for anything. Lamb, lobster,
tail and all. This infinite
martyrdom between us: how,
on another shore, my mother could only
afford to eat meat once a year,
on her birthday. Boiled rice

with sweet potatoes: her comfort.
My grandmother salvages the sweet
peels, brown like the bark
of a tree I have loved for years. I worry
this recipe will be in *Food & Wine*.
Epicurean discoveries of "peasant" food.
My comfort: stir-fried tomato
and egg, appears in _____.
Do not look this up.
But the frontier beams and thickens
each glowing intestine, pink and
pinker still: *Comfort for you, comfort for all!*
Do not look this up.

On TV, I hear about the dense
understory of trees with living,
thread-like fungi: mycelium.
The unrelenting pursuit
of it. Living. In the shower,
my mother wrings out water
from her hair, growing wavy
as she grows older. We can
all see. Her hair, how
sound travels. And the ocean,
waving back, terror
tucked away for now.

THE CACTUS

I've never planned on being weak.
(I thought of myself as a cactus,
flooded with sun and armor that
could strike an arm or eye. I know
how to hold my own arm, to hold
my breath when spirits pass, as they do,
trailing after a desert rat. Or at least
I thought such things.) I think of
your fear of losing me, I think
of a seal who can't make it back
to water, its stupid whistling cry
(the leaving, most of all, a shimmering
plague). Who would dare to admit it:
the buckling over, the cold bones
of some other man's hands,
the sleep for sleep's sake,
(for no reason but to wilt each spike,
my armor plucked, how vulgar—
a naked porcupine). Here, at this gutting
hour, I ask myself: What have you done?
Do you even know? I know I am not
a sight to see. (Even deer move around
me, not looking.) Plums from a tree
fall and hit me straight on the head
(the deer keep on not looking).
That wobble, that wreck: I have
tried again. I let down my hair.
I lugged out my terror. The exhaustion,
ad infinitum: throw everything you
know into the ocean (and watch
it come back to you, different).

WHAT I TELL MYSELF AFTER WAKING UP WITH FISTS

Tired of fighting — undo your armor — stuck to your ribs like a good, fat meal — undo the gristle — knuckled in the prior — in gluttonous, bee-drunk June — calling back what was never — there, can you believe it, your mother says, a man — can cry over a dog's dead body — but won't look you in the eye — facts multiply like the arms of an aloe plant — spears of fact: you have never done what has been done to you — fact: each leaving radiates with alien light – each apology: an overdressed salad you will eat – nevertheless — vow: do not wash your face at night — let all your hexes seep into your pores — vow: uncurl yourself from weaponry — for: you know what it feels like — an arrow in the arm — rustling in splinters — allow: light what uses your strength against you — fawn, fear, or wreck — each fist somersaulting in what knuckle — ruthless: write a poem for love —before love can even exist

I PUT ON MY FUR COAT

And leave a bit of ankle to show.
I take off my shoes and make myself
comfortable. I defrost a chicken
and chew on the bone. In public,
I smile as wide as I can and everyone
shields their eyes from my light.
At night, I knock down nests off
telephone poles and feel no regret.
I greet spiders rising from underneath
the floorboards, one by one. Hello,
hello. Outside, the garden roars
with ice. I want to shine as bright
as a miner's cap in the dirt dark,
to glimmer as if washed in fish scales.
Instead, I become a balm and salve
my daughter, my son, the cold mice
in the garage. Instead, I take the garbage
out at midnight. I move furniture away
from the wall to find what we hide.
I stand in the center of every room
and ask: Am I the only animal here?

LESSONS ON LESSENING

I wake to the sound of my neighbors upstairs as if they are bowling.

And maybe they are, all pins and love fallen over.
I lay against my floor, if only to feel that kind of affection.

What I've learned, time and again—
get up. You cannot have what they have.

And the eyes of a dead rat can't say anything.

In Jersey, the sink breaks and my mother keeps a bucket
underneath to save water for laundry.

A trickle of water is no joke. I've learned that.
Neither is my father, wielding a knife in starlight.

I was taught that everything and everyone is self-made.

That you can make a window out of anything if you want.
This is why I froze insects. To see if they will come back to life.

How I began to see each day: the sluice of wings.
Get up. The ants pouring out of the sink, onto my arms in dish heavy water.

My arms: branches. A swarm I didn't ask for.

No one told me I'd have to learn to be polite.
To let myself be consumed for what I cannot control.

I must return to my younger self. To wearing my life
like heavy wool, weaved in my own weight.

To pretend not to know when the debtors come to collect.

AFTER MY FATHER LEAVES, MY MOTHER OPENS
THE WINDOWS

to let the smoke out, to air out

each promise, each day my father

disappears in Atlantic City.

A pigeon flies in and rejoices

with us. We dance like hornets

stinging the ugliest of babies.

Praise the breath! Praise Orange Glo

cleaner! I help her carry my father's

floral armchair, covered in cigarette

burns, down to the basement and

shove it into a corner we can all forget.

Decades before, in another country,

in 1967, my grandmother has no windows

to open. No pigeon, no basement, no

daughter to call her own. In 1967,

my grandmother sneaks a cigarette in lousy

moonlight and coughs up a cricket.

All around her, the Red Army moves

through mud, boots of spackle

and shine. Her husband will disappear

soon in Hong Kong, in the rattle of trams

and trash heaps. In the moonlight,

her cheeks are blistered plums—

plums my mother places on our kitchen

windowsill to dry out. Some kind

of medicine that could cure the distance

between all of us. This stone fruit,

blessed in sun and open air.

DREAM OF THE LOPSIDED CROWN

I have this dream where I am the Daughter of the Machinist.
My father, balancing pipes that lead to other pipes, dropping
a marble ball. Precision as love, without remainders, without
the toothy excess of spiral-bound notebooks. I cut love clean.

Instead, I am the Daughter of the Gambler. *Who is winning this
staring contest?* I ask my father. *I dare you to blink!* Slumped slug,
he spills all the chips on the table and says nothing, always
nothing. *Chirp, chirp,* goes the robin, Robber of Dreams.

All around me, Atlantic City butters itself with dinner rolls, roiling
ocean bilge. No one looks me in the eye. Here is the Daughter,
spun in boardwalk cotton candy, puke-perfect. Here is the Father,
saying, *I am your father.* Village after village, fishmongers walk away

from their fish, drawn to city stupor. Dream of the Dung Beetle,
I soothe. Of its celestial turns, simple machinations in muck.

With each celestial turn, each match, I am mucked, soothed not—
no tooth under no pillow. I gnaw on a spare rib to teethe myself,
delicious. Dream of the Baby Owl, twisting its bright eye onto
you. When I was born, I did not cry or blink, a Telescope Doll,

spittle-spun and talcum-tossed. My mother told me she's the only
beauty left in this world. I knocked my gavel in agreement. *Hear,
hear.* Song of Justice, Just Enough. Today, the planets gnaw on
their nails in smoke, exhausted. I wipe CO_2 from my memory,

in a circular motion, waving hello. In a photograph, my mother
cradles me in New York and I: shaking a fist in front of a statue
of a white general who did not go to jail for murder. Across
the street: Casino Buses of Lost Dreams arrive in Chinatown

with red cigarette streamers. Here, the ghosts cry so loudly you
can see their breath in alleyways, winter wailing down to rats.

Rats seethe in alleyway walls, where winter cannot fall down
sooner. My brother, born in the blue flame of February,
is my mirror kin. Together, we kick everything in sight
to see better. Ant hill, MSG bin, box of plastic cutlery

clanging a xylophone avant-garde. We raise seashells to
our ears and hear nothing but garbage trucks lifting all
that we waste but want. *Crush crap,* the Dinosaur of
Garbage gobbles. Together, the Restaurant Babies refill

napkin and sauce containers like regurgitating bird food.
We sing of duck sauce and chili and straws pulled down
by levers, levitating in tubular innovation. Customers
furnish their mouths with lacquered loins, a pork

procession. Dream of the Country That Shall Not Be
Named, coins in clouds held over our heads like carrots.

Head in the clouds, I coined a name: Hellish Careless Rot.
What I called the garden my father smoked in, seeds of
ash and fire spit. Cilantro stems under boots of drunk
men demanding payback for oceans they've crossed,

convinced the Ocean crossed them. *Cross my heart,* my
father swears, eyes as red as a rabbit, Grazer of Nothing.
Tomatoes roll down sidewalks, little splats of startling
summer. Dream of My Heart Rolling Away, state by

state. Late July, my grandmother clips green vines with
her claws, wears it as jade. The garden simmers in brackish
brown slush. Rot like armpits, rot like lizard eyes. I dream
of string beans so long, they lineage. My Mother the Gardener

digs deep like every worm I've known. She overturns the soil,
the Living freshly furrowed. *I want a vegetal love,* she lulls.

She loves all that is living: wants fresh fur, a lullaby of vegetables
to sing her aching bones to sleep. My mother stretches snakelike,
hissing at machines she furnishes with envelopes. Her body over-
worked, my love flying around her like a bat. Frantic flight, I echo,

Won't you take a day off? Dream of Labor as Love. *Overtime is time
and a half,* the Half Moon coos. My Bat Love: her kindly blind
kin. Equations of the Equator calculate. Night shift after night
shift equals sedimentary sleep. At Pimple Dusk, my brother

inspects stubble on his chin, looks like the Father as Adolescent
Idol. Year after year, we watch banks being built on ancient
ground, money sprouting rabbit ears and rivers receding in
recession. My father blinks a bottle away, wobbles in his wonder,

Where is the Daughter? If by mountain, canyon, forest, or heart
ambled. *Daughter, I have this dream where I say what I mean, first.*

WHEN YOU DIED

I went to the library to find you.
I stained a book on Maoist-era politics.
With the tomato soup I had microwaved earlier.
And it crusted the page like a ridge.
In the Grand Canyon or the surface of Mars in love.
Or an army uniform cratered.
In the blood of others.
I am sorry. I do not know which analogy.
To use, what to say to the fact of it all.
36 million deaths from 1958 to 1962.
Estimated. What no one talks.
About, called "epidemic," not starvation.
At my grandmother's grave in Jersey, the ground.
Was as soft as a perfectly poached egg.
And I almost plunged my arms into the soil.
To touch her—her purple jade bracelet shining.
Like the ring of an undiscovered planet.
Or a truant yam among all this empty clay. All.
This empty. I am sorry to give you.
That hope. I did not plunge my arms into the earth.
I held these Safeway flowers, dipped in bleach and blue.
These wrinkled petal faces, drifting in gasoline.
Air. This yawning gap between us all.
The more things change, what remains the same?

You can have it all:

dried cabbage butterfly;

clay to draw out

impurities; rice straw,

how to roll it up

in a ball to make bao,

(can it hold); fresh locust

if they come (call them

to come, call them to

flutter in your ribs);

termites along the gums,

an antennae for

another day; double-cooked

rice; decade-old ox bones

dug up, crushed,

and boiled. You can have

this. The need to ingest

anything. Even the interior

redness of stars.

A river thawed just enough

to see the eels underneath

but not enough to touch them.

When you died, the husks of insects

hung about in the wind: little suits

of distinction. When you died,

lettuce wilted each time

you carried your brother home

at night, his hair tangled

with manure as if he were a crop

in need of growth. When you died,

you knew the different levels of relief:

the moon follows another day,

another day hollows out

bowl by bowl. And isn't that enough?

Nothing is for naught. Or so

you were told and scolded by armies

of ants. When you died, this hand

prodding your back was not your country,

not your youth, rosy at the cheeks

from the sun, striking at noon.

Was not what you curled toward

in the early morning fog and fury,

your breath sent: skyward.

Were you hungry? Were your feet clean

      or covered in dirt? Who cut your hair?

Did the oil in your hair smell of gasoline?

      Corn? Mint leaves? The fields of wheat,

were they as tall as a building in a city

      swarming with pigeons in your dream of it?

Was I a pigeon in this city in your dream? Were you

      hungry when dreaming? Were there ants

in the rice? Did their feet wash the rice clean?

      Don't you like your rice clean? Can you touch

the inside of my ear and say it feels like the inside of your ear?

      Like a rock you kept in your breast pocket,

from the red morning's empty haul? Was the rock

      you cleaned pink? Were you full and pink and

tall, your feet a marble slab I could wipe clean?

I don't want to tell you how Chinese people died lining up for a corn oil sale, trampled from the weight of desperation and the ambered cake of the sun, sugaring above.

Or how bad men have held their hands around my neck, greedy as a fish eating another fish's eggs.

What I want to tell you: I am a good daughter. I repeat this until my lungs puncture little star-like holes.

Constellations of my devotion. I am trying. A daughter, breathing. I listen to the story. Of you collapsing in the kitchen, of my grandmother finding you, holding my infant mother. Of mucus pouring out of your mouth like so many slugs. I am trying hard not to place my cold hand on your forehead, to ease something devouring you, inside out.

The mouth should not sprout mushrooms and if so, I would not blame your neighbors for eating them, for lifting your earthly tubers to their faces for a kiss.

Researching, I am afraid of phrases like "edema" and "the euphoric stage." Of poisonous food substitutes from the government. What the stomach does with too much water and nothing else. Who can turn into a bottom-feeder fish like that?

I loosen a balloon into the sky and it floats between two waterlogged storm clouds.

What to do in the world of the living.

I've always eaten what was given to me and then I'd eat it again. Chewed and chewed until everything coated my interior self with a silk sheen. Greasing a pan. 脂肪, fat.

The smear of oil along my arms, duck leg after duck leg. Bones in heaps, in stews, in swelling heat. So many string beans, they sprout from my ears and warble my hearing. I'm trying to listen.

My mother fills an empty can of soup with water and swirls it, until each speck of oil catches. How beautiful, this twinkling tin. I have always loved what most people throw away: broccoli stems, fish heads, the white of green onions and its dangling foot like an anemone, the rat tail of a radish. I dream of boiling the salty shells of pistachios. Of gorging myself with compost, slick with nutrients.

It was definitely not fate. It was hukou and forced collectivization. It was the face of a man you'll never see. How he dined on fish eggs, briny pearls. No one's fate to eat old bird droppings, cotton, clay. What can be plucked from corpses, roses in May. I told you I was afraid.

Not fate.

I ate and ate and ate. I am your good daughter.

In the Pacific Northwest, two deer stare back at me in the woods, their antlers pulled up toward the moon like arms reaching up. They watch me carefully and can barely breathe through their hot, velvet noses. They know. Their fear trills around them, spitting dew on ferns. I want to slice their bellies open, to gather this otherworldly meat. To feed you until your eyes shine back and the slugs recede from your mouth. And when you've had enough, I'll drape you in their hides, ever-warm.

It takes some time, but the balloon arrives to take you away. For a proper burial, for a cornucopia afterlife. The balloon lifts your small, emptied body up with its one tendril and you hover above the floor, in disbelief.

You whisper: Whose ear is pressed to this floor?

I bow, ever-full: Your good son's good daughter's good daughter.

Did you wonder who was coming home?
No loyal dog, no father, no mother in clean

pressed linen, no river to wash away
the dirt from your eyes? Know this:

your eyes are large enough to build
a ditch in. If the sky is red, stay inside.

Do not look anyone in the eye or
you will turn into a pot. No one wants

to be a pot to cook nothing with.

Did you see roses blocking the street?
No? The air wasn't full of thorns?

The rot: not red and slug-sick?
Take care of the cabbage, even in the rain.

Take heed of your little brother,
wean him with a stick of sugarcane.

No sugarcane? Not even in your
neighbor's cupboard? Remember what belongs

to someone else does not belong
to you. Give your brother your thumb

instead; keep your nails long.

Did you have a name and did the army
take it away? Did you try to hold

onto your name? An armful of emptiness
is better than nothing. You do not

believe me? Tell me then: what is the use
of making sense during a time

like this, during a red sky like that,
dangling about like a sweet

slice of meat you want to devour?

Five years of fireflies in oil; five years of ants gnawing

through red flags; five years of pockmarked suns, your face:

each ray, each sweltering August; five years of unraveling,

hair loosening from your crown like a rotten tooth;

five years of how easy it is to split a frog in two; five

years of pollen in your mouth, that bitter buzzing;

one year of leeches along the spine, fattening; two years:

are rats good to eat? Another year: sun-licked pots;

your birth year: the cold bones of a stranger's hand;

the quiet year: no one wants to look at a gaping

fish, swallowing water endlessly; the sixth year:

to place these flowers on or in the graves?

Hunger travels like a bee—always moving,

    always at the ready. What hunger knows,

you do not. To funnel mud from water,

    do not use your mouth. Count the red ants

along your toes. Count the length of time

    it takes them to reach your hair, to make

a home. Half a century later, I count the apples

    that fall from trees. I know I can't stop them

from rotting on the ground. I can't go back and

    give them to you. Even the squirrels here

won't have it. Sometimes there is nothing to say or

    give at all. Sometimes an awful feeling comes

over me like a cavity I can't fill. Like a beetle

    I crushed out of fury and fear and cannot

resurrect, cannot redress in armor. And then I see

    my mother, picking meat from the spine

of a fish carefully, as if she were pulling a tick out,

    careful to mind the entire body. This frugality,

this tender grazing—our relation. My mother,

    your future child: a bee that prefers the ocean.

Half a century later,
I am checking and rechecking
an egg to make sure
it's still good. I press
my nose against the rotten
planet, cold as a half-sung
song. Halved, I am
more than your weight,
still. When you died,
where were your teeth?
Where was your breath?
Breathe on this window for me.
Let me draw flowers on it.
Half a century later, geese tap
at my yard as if checking
for solid ground. Do you
think about twisting its fat
neck? Why do I think about
twisting its fat neck, about
that lovely puncture?
When you died, the guards
shouted industry and agriculture
into the air, their breath humid
enough to grow a mole.
I buy lettuce from the grocery
store and wash nothing.
When you died, you gulped
at the air, you slept with both
eyes open. You dreamt of
the fattening dough of the sky,
of geese singing in the future.
Loss sat in a living room
you didn't have. Loss settled in
like heavy whipping cream,
like a new kind of mud.
Over a century later,
my teeth keep sharpening
for something to come.
I eat and eat and eat again.
Year after year, I leave eggs
by your grave, by ground
I can't seem to find.

In Beijing, the sky is a smoke monster you can't cure anything in. In Tiananmen Square, an LCD screen projects the sunrise. Pixels promise something the sky cannot. Stunning gasps under face masks, made small enough for babies too. Paper nests to keep out contaminants.

In Seattle, your son cures pork belly, leathered and wrinkled like his face refusing memory. The belly puckers on white paper towels along the sill. Absorbent two-ply, they bloom a watercolor of fat.

Here, thick strips of pork sunbathe in evergreen air. The strips look like bark, like driftwood I gather in the basket of my arms. To feel closer to something tossed, something settled.

Mud in the belly, my mother says when something doesn't sit quite right.

Your son, my grandfather, lives in a studio apartment in the Central District. Subsidized government housing for the elderly, mostly Chinese. In the courtyard, grandfathers in thin white shirts sit and smoke cigarettes, smoke wrapping their branch arms. A Japanese maple unfolds carelessly, an umbrella of low burgundy

ash. When I walk down the hallways of the housing complex, I see the red plastic sandals of every grandmother and grandfather, decorated with cartoon tigers and full-mane bears, holding balloons or firecrackers. I see steam rising from underneath every door, breath and fog. All at once,

the lids of their rice cookers open

                                caverns of salt

        & plenty

Plastic machinery. Growing up, our rice cooker was painted with peonies and cherry blossoms. Plugged into a wall, an eye socket, a button pressed to cook or warm. Grease and dust along the cord. A rice paddle like a wide tongue depressor, table salt shaken like dandruff from my unwashed hair.

What I want to tell you: In another life, there is a button to press to cook and warm rice. A circle glows as red as a growing army, just to reassure you:

You will eat.

Once, when I was four, I poured Carnation condensed milk all over my face. I was as white as I'll ever be. Eyelashes of cream, I blinked on, too ghostly for my own good.

I admit too:
        I've pitched eggs
                into parking lots

    just because
        I liked the sound:
                        the sumptuous splat

    of sun (I am
                sorry for drooling). I
                    know: what a shame, what

    a waste, this hasty
        child: not mine. And

what a taste too, that oil
                spooled in gracious
                        gravel.

1959: stoves dismantled. The government orders comrades to melt pots and pans in a makeshift furnace. This act of melting iron, how you imagine the corona of the sun. Metallic gray, lava sludge. Diseased plasma, unsettling. Disappearing in your slivering gut like cold sardines. Little eyeballs in the throat.

I want to tell you: I dated a vegetarian for two years and he was as tall as a factory. When he went out to dinner with my family, table heaped with meat heads (how

ugh) my mother said she was also vegetarian growing up. Meaning poor, meaning scallions sprouting out of everyone's mouths. If you were lucky, there would at least be sprouting.

As a teenager, my mother worked in a factory a few hours away from her village, embroidering luxurious birds: peacocks, herons, swans. Anything but pigeons.

I close my eyes and imagine my mother's factory collapsing, pin needles
                                        studding the sky.

                                        I have this strange feeling.

I've written this before. I've always been writing to you, even before I was born.

Everything reminds me of you and I don't even know what your face looks like. Your ears, are they as large as mine? Bats in an otherwise cavernous world?

Along the Puget Sound, I break sand dollars in half and revel in how easy it is, like breaking apart an almond cracker. To break that which is already dead. Easy, to not pummel bone. To not stir the dust into a spackle of soup. I can't bear to look at live sand dollars, their little feet trilling underneath, half-black half-purple, in the very process of dying. It takes time.

How long does the process take?

On and on and on. Actual mud, actual belly.

What went wrong: a wrongdoing.

I read about taro scrubbing, about villagers accused of stealing. To come clean, officials took turns beating them. How it all sounds like a game: ring around the roses, scrubbing skin to ashes, to all fall down. I falter on the page. What should be yours and wasn't? What was swallowed whole? What roots, what ground to hold?

To become a ghost, I see through milk as thick as whatever pours out of your mouth. Sediment, sludge. Organ milk, floral and fecund. Budding bile returning to soil. Carnation, coronation. What pours out of the body, malnourished. Shame, I admit, to turn away in order

to look. I finish each heaping grain, glossy-
eyed, and heart

hurtling to end. A bowl cracks open then.

What I am learning: beware of the light you cannot see.

AFTER HE TRAVELS THROUGH ASH, MY GRANDFATHER SPEAKS

I have grown so many black hairs—it's miraculous really. They sprout like seaweed, like the spindles of a newborn hairbrush. No one told me my hair would still grow, especially not in my ears. Somehow, my hearing is even better—like the wind along fat ferns. I hear like that, feeling the cold in the howling *o*'s of your questions. Can you believe it, how I've forgotten the sounds of cars, the sounds of buses leaving without me in huffs of impatience? I don't remember what a broken toothpick sounds like or how Chinese soap operas loop like precious snakes along my apartment's walls. I can only hear the vowels of your questions, your fists curling and uncurling in sleep, the low rush of wind along ferns so tall—they must be pulled up by the sky

THE FRONTIER

The frontier fauns over
signs that declare who
to vote for, who to keep
out and who to (lose all)
love. Printed on demand,
sold and stamped at the co-op
and the roadside gas station
I swerved and stomped
a slushie in. Signs peeling
like the good skin of a good
onion, prongs sinking in
fertilizer, grass. When distressed,
the frontier points to the sign
of no time, greased in
grudges: we reserve the right
to refuse service. Can flip
this table and say: *No dinner
for you!* The clanging plates
singing in fried potato
air. How my brother and I
used to make secret signs
like doves wrestling in our hands
when someone says something
not right, when a white man
makes the sign of the cross
staring at our mother's legs.
Doves diving into headlock:
how anger sinks and singes
in our feverish palms.

In this country, an owl won't attack
what looks them in the eye. Talons
straight in the back, a swoop and
steal, three steps behind. I look
behind me for many reasons:
the frontier creeping in
at the edges: bougainvillea,

shoreline bilge, algae. Creeping
critters, how men trill
behind me like wasps smelling
my hair or wet dogs who dove
into pitiful winter water
or ambulances of unnecessary
emergency or the fog following
any hot breath or manifest
destiny sloshed on canyon
carvings. Sick. All of the above:
my circling head, omniscient
eye on creep duty. I look
behind me to keep close tabs
on my enemies. The darts
of my eyes: poison frogs
in slime spurs, gargantuan
rhubarb leaves, nightshade roots
gargling. You better watch
where you crawl, creeper.
I am far from done.

I HAUL A HOUSE OUT OF THE BAY

There is something about digging my arms into mud
as if I'm trying to find all the loves I've lost—dragging

each burrowed foot, each ventricle in bivalves. How I
tender the spit of the bay, murk trilling my arm hairs.

The jutting claw of a crab eyes me from its windowless
home. You and me both, I want to say. Mud buries in

nail beds, my bending heart furnishes fat hulls through
weeds to sustain me—how my grandfather squatted

as wide as a kite and dug to feed his children, the shells
ringing along my mother's mouth otherwise songless.

I pull clam after clam from the slumping earth and toss
it into a bucket, clanging a warning for those who've

wronged us. The tide lulls in lopsided adoration. I haul
these houses, my eyes dripping with clams. Salt air slops

along my gums. Punctuated with specks of sea grease,
I bend to turn the earth again, the earth muscling against

me. Each hinge, each ghost—opening. In the murky slough
of day, I grit and dig, singing our long decay to sleep.

HOW TO NOT BE AFRAID OF EVERYTHING

How to not punch everyone in the face.

How to not protect everyone's eyes from

my own punch. I have been practicing

my punch for years, loosening my limbs.

My jaw unhinged creates a felony I refuse

to go to court for. The fat of spam pools

in the sun, reminding me of my true feelings.

My feelings leak from my ear like a bad cold

in a bad storm. Stars huddle in a corner,

little radiators sweating out their fear.

An opossum reaches his arm up from a porch.

I hold onto his arm for a little while, for

a little warmth. At night, my subterranean eye

begins to rove. Song of the underground,

song of the rat tribe. I see my mother in

an apron splattered with viscera I will eat

for dinner. To gut her work out, to work

her guts out. Can we talk about privilege?

Can I say I always look behind me? I always

look behind me. I always take a step forward

like I'm about to save myself from toppling

over. The bare bones of it: some of us know

that spoiled meat still counts as protein.

That a horse's neck snaps from the weight

of what it carries, from the weight of what

we give it to carry. I bundle up a sack of

clouds, empty of rain and fear and lightning.

WHAT IS LOVE IF NOT ROT

I've been watching videos of rotting oranges on time-lapse again — it's barely noticeable at first — the pores begin to grow, craters of no importance — after 14 days, the skin thins out, rice-paper thin, wind-thin, loneliness-thin — at 15 days, spots bloom like a newborn galaxy or a bald buzzard — circling, a shadow returning winter's wail — the skin puckers in on itself, all chimney ash, all brain-matter mold — the middle like touching a young organ — slobbering milk and mud — a pedestal of goldenrod flora at 17 days — at 20 days, moss lumbers up and through — continents growing along this orb — thickening at 22 days like cotton lint from the dryer, like fur, a sheepskin cloud, like my mother — an animal in her own right, expanding — now, the color phlegm-yellow, poor-yellow — growing smaller and smaller by 25 days — collapsing upon itself like curled fists — how I sleep at night, returning to heartbreak after heartbreak – fruit flies fluttering about like snow — what is holding it up still, what is keeping it here, how can I bear — to watch it — how can I — liquefy by 45 days, wolfish in citrus murk — ever-shrinking like every grandparent I've ever held hands with — at 85 days, how to hold this slush of glittering bees — trapped in no worldly amber —

THE BEET

The first time I sliced open a beet
I tumbled backward, a useless green top
not knowing what to do with all of it:
the drenched cutting board, the organ spill
getting everywhere like the loans
I owe. I thought of lava thick as a tongue,
of my father's ruined jaw
misshapen like a novice ceramicist's bowl,
his teeth knocked out post gambling
brawl. I remembered singing
a lullaby for all our jaws and
scrubbing my grandmother's feet
raw, each toe curling toward tomato vines
and water spinach legs. Naturally,
I thought of my heart, that trembling
water tower. I wanted love.
It would occur to me, later,
in the center slice, how the beet
reminded me of undressing in front of you
in the weeks before you left, the nonchalance
of each shorn sleeve, as if opening
and closing a window to air
out an apartment that held too many lives.
The beet's anemone foot, trilling, the whittled
foot of my love, dragging. How I've forgotten
all the edible parts. The darker pink rings,
tree rings, years in neon lit upheaval.
Who told you anything is permanent?
How generous this bloodletting.
How elementary, my cheek against the root,
beet-stamped, clownish in my blush.

WRONG JUNE

I spent all afternoon trying
to match some animal's tracks

to my own. I cannot make
good use of my time.

I cannot declare buoyancy.
I have been loitering

in backyard sheds again.
These days, there is moss growing

in all the wrong places.
What does it mean

that I've been willing
my white hairs in?

That I've been staring
at the microwave for hours?

Judgment cuts through me
like a magician sawing

a woman in half. Like shearing
a sleeping lamb, loosened

of its woven weight.
My debacle of self:

a cold fried egg
you can't refurbish.

Let it be known:
no one wants to know

about the woman who coughs.
No one wants to dangle

about like a loose doorknob.
We should all turn away

from the spider stretching its legs,
feeling a crime coming on.

Away from the neighbor boy
who pisses on a fire

to put it out. To render the fat
of judgment, I'll drain it

and keep it in a jar. A pile of flies
will gather in the jar.

This buzzing cloud,
my wrong over June.

THE EGG

held to the nose
took me back to the field
where my mother held
a chicken's neck down
with thin branch arms
and struck its neck—
that whimpering bridge
from brain to heart—
with a cleaver as wide
as a flooded river.
Her reflection in the shine
of it—her yolk-swamped
eyes, the speckled pluck
of her brow, measuring
the animal's past life.
How it would stir
in the mucus of the hull,
touch its beak to the cool
crater, testing it, how
my brother and I yearned
to lick the sugar spackle
of an Easter egg but
were told: No, not yet—

UNKINDLY KIND

When thou weep'st, unkindly kind,
My life's blood doth decay.
—John Donne

A caterpillar clings to my window, its little trilling
feet sucked against the glass. How lucky I am to be
this admired. How I've waited years to be clung to,
even temporarily. Stay awhile, I plead. Its red-furred
head peels up, as if listening for danger. Not done,
I touch the glass, press my finger to its swaying undertow.
The wind flares in absolutes, combing a chill across
its too-soft body, which turns away from me like every
man I've slept with, slowly and surely. Maybe, by morning,
I could collect enough of so-and-so's breath to sustain me
for the coming months of so many ghost arms. Unkindly
kind, to love that which does not love me back. Fresh out
of lack, I flop like a goldfish in my bed, sorrow stung
with so little honey. I break open a claw of aloe vera
and smear it all over my body, toes and all. I shine out
like this, stupidly green. I spit into a cup and spit again to let
myself know that there's still so much within me. My heart,
a slickened thing. In my solitude, I listen to the song of
the dryer, spinning warmth. The caterpillar turns back
on the glass, inches closer, romanced by the lute of the linen.
Oh dear. Oh decay. That is what it has come to: making a metaphor
out of nothing, again. I must be lifted out of this, helicoptered
to some better place, quick. My mother calls me in this pink
pulse of heartache, reminds me that the river only rises
in one direction. *I don't know what you mean*, I say,
tell me what you mean! But then she roars so loudly,
I have no choice but to join the racket and wrestle
out my lungs. This is not where I thought I'd be.
Roaring in a room where something is about to heal.

NOTES FOR THE INTERIOR

The nightly news clings to the wall like mold.
Spores tumble about the air, headed straight for my mouth.
It is easy to be nice to someone, my mother says.
Like cutting a block of tofu in half.
No gristle, no grit, no fat to chew through.
And yet: this country full of fear, my heart full of fever.
When people walk past me, they spit up their lunch.
I speak to you from this crack in the sidewalk, absorbing the spit.
Maybe I want nice things: napkins instead of toilet paper.
A rat after a soak in a mountain spring.
A glass of honey water in full health.
I lurch forward, rage blooming in my bones.
Magnolia and marrow.
A fire burns in the rain, miles away.
The embers swim about like bees in the back of our throats.

My mother tosses our secrets into a well.
She lets them rot over with moss and ant shit.
The house is dirty on the second floor.
Why clean what no one cares to see?
In the evening, crows walk along the roofs of cars, deliberating.
In the morning, I pull hair from my mouth: my mother's and mine.
Thin black snakes in the flour bin.
A storm passes through my hometown like a late parade.
Confetti on a slug is not as welcoming as you would think.
I raise my arms to the sky and begin loitering in the air.
The crows have reached a decision.
They declare: *Leave any country that has a name.*

On the news, the word "enemy" is repeated so many times, it rises to the top of a
mountain.
Enemies softly gather in the clouds, cumulus.
What is the use of shouting when no one looks you in the eye?
Today, we can be forgiven for so many things.

Like mistaking my name for another, for vice, and vice versa.

> I know it is a luxury to not know what your army looks like.

The army could just be a field of dandelions.

> Under which flag do we gather such bouquets?

I think: if only I can find my father's left lung, my missing family, that extra ration.

> Everything will be whole.

And yet: the fluorescence of hospital trash frightens me.

> In kitchens everywhere, potato skins are being thrown away.

Heaps and heaps of starchy blight.

To avoid suspicion, erase your genealogy one branch at a time.

> In the evening, wash mud from your feet and pat to dry.

Welcome loneliness like a painting you never intended to look at.

> Become an eyesore or a sorry father returning home to find the locks changed.

Keep changing the locks; keep the front door swept clean.

> No ants, no beetles, no leaves blown in from enemies.

Countries away, a village drains a lake for carp.

> Fish flap about in foggy water, percussive milk.

Tell me: is this my army?

> Each day, the sun shaves itself away, sliver by sliver.

Diminishment reminds me that all bones must be removed from memory.

> My aunt pulls a fish bone from her throat: no harm, no foul.

It is easy to be nice to someone, I tell myself.

Once, I watched a video of The Ice Man sitting in ice water for two hours.

> Everyone congratulated this act of defying nature.

Why would anyone welcome danger into their lives?

> The heat from a fox's snarl rises.

At night, the undercarriage of a bridge loosens.

> A butterfly crawls into a chip bag.

During a meeting, I overhear someone say: *I'm not that far from a criminal act.*

> I pull my sweater over my head and back again just to feel a shift.

When my mother chased the man who tried to take her purse, what was she thinking?

> Pure certainty, as tall as wheat we can hide in.

If revenge is an occupation, let our queen know where to go to work.

66

Light bursts above our heads, a prism of custard yellow.

But really: someone forgot to pay the electric bill.

Was it you? Our reflex: to ignore the knock at the door.

In this part of the country, there is no elm, no magnolia, no pretty, pretty begonia.

Crows kick up dust from the statue of a political figure in the square.

The ocean spits back a thousand dead jellyfish, glowing still.

If only I can find my lost language, my brother's rotten molars, my missing family members.

I hunch over in caution, in wind as white as a wall.

Funeral white as white as a face drawn toward a coffin, a blanched butterfly.

How terrible, to have elegies already prepared.

How terrible, to get up and walk away from a life.

A life neither yours nor mine, and yet this sickness sprouting.

Dirt in the gut: the incomprehensibility of it.

How many people died during the Great Leap Forward?

A woman in the public library hushes me with her eyes.

Cumulus clouds form in the white.

I lob industrialization away from me.

Pots and pans fill the air like cherry blossoms.

I open my mouth as wide as a bridge carrying people carrying lumber.

Today, I read on the news that Chinese people are buying up fresh air from Canada.

I tell myself to breathe through my brain.

When he was little, my brother folded pieces of paper into a boat.

Migration as pulp, as bleached buoyancy.

What is the use of returning and to what?

At night, my mother stirs a pot of broth and her face smells like chicken bones.

I try to get close to her face, snout-close, but she swats me away.

There are some things I know I shouldn't do.

I have trouble picking things up from the ground without biting them.

Death cap mushrooms, this raving beetle, one hundred dandelions.

Me: gnawing at the air.

My mother arrived in New York in 1983.

A worm rises from a head of cabbage, announcing its presence.

Good-bye oxen, good-bye sugarcane, good-bye dirt under the nails.

When no one looks, she picks up loose change from the sidewalk.

I ate an egg and cheese sandwich today and it fell onto my chest.

Embarrassment lessens when you get older.

No side step from the mud, no turning away from roadkill and its soft clumped fur.

These days, I welcome the mere fact of it all.

Yes, there is a bucket full of batteries in the garage.

The truth is, you never know when something might be of use later.

My grandfather tells me he will die soon or: *What is wrong with you, why can't you marry?*

In the future, people will say that I was so lonely, I married a phantom limb.

Silver crown, silver crown, silver crown, I sing to myself.

My body, this ever-growing mass: a sea cucumber and its ribbons of guts.

A boat bellows in the Puget Sound and I bellow back.

A bellow like slashing tires with my teeth.

A bellow to say: *You think I am too quiet? Speak a little louder?*

I snarl the sound into everyone's face until they say they want no more: *Uncle, uncle!*

My uncle died and no one told my grandmother.

Silence as a long, wandering sigh.

She was pruning a pear tree as the procession drove by.

To carry something you don't want to carry.

Winter melons balanced on your crown.

It is easy to be nice to someone, my mother tells me.

If they don't cross you first.

Horseradish held along the tongue is a good test.

Will you pass or fail or fall over trying?

I draw *X*'s in the air, in the route of bees I know to fear.

THE LONG LABORS

My grandmother said it was going to be long — as long as you can hold your lineage — depending on how long you can hold your tongue — as long as your tongue can wrap around the pit — of some stolen stone fruit —as long as you can hide your pitter-patter face — glued in sun-split splinters – lengthening shadows as long as your face — longing to be mirrored back — back to your daughter your mother your grandmother — freckle by freckle — furnished forever across — the long loaming haul —   Collapsed in a pool of spit — my mouth over papers — raccoon doctorate — luxurious loser with thin branch fingers — no meat in the palm — no muscle in the bending — the farmer in me is atrophying — the cook the factory seamstress the clerk the mother in me is pooling out — all that I come from — all that I owe to them — what is left of me — what is — me: professorial rat — book leavened and maddened in meetings — chewing at my desk on a frozen anything — microwave spun and splattered on lessons — wondering who packaged this — who spooned this glacial sauce into this plastic hull — whose hands whose daughter does she look like me does she like dancing in the gloaming — funneled into my greedy mouth — I: daughter of long labors — I: knock-off half-price guilt — I: impossible imposter big words big words — trying to prove what — and to whom — I wait to be seated at a restaurant — a white person enters and orders from me — "I want sweet and sour chicken but without bell peppers and brown rice" — and I almost take it down —
                    In the twelfth hour of nightshift overtime — my mother gobbles the air of the facility — mouth opening a cavern or a bowhead whale or a sinkhole — gobbling up its oxygen its nitrogen its argon its skin its hair dust its swirling smog — collecting time collecting benefits — her eyes so baggy they carry a leaking pack of chicken breasts — she had planned to cook tonight for us — but look at the break room clock she is out of time and now — they will surely go bad — what a waste at $1.50 a pound — she returns to her station rubs tiger balm and lavender oil along her wrists and hands — chews dried ginger to keep awake — the root of herself sharpening salivating — reapplies pink lipstick swivels the tube upwards — rituals of resilience — feeds letters to machines churning intestinal noise — electricity bills and love letters and baby photos and magazines ladies who lunch will take to the salon and credit card limited time offers and reminders from the dentist and supermarket weeklies and postcards from Oahu "you wouldn't believe how blue the water how restful how peaceful bring the whole family next time" — ginger chew ginger chew —   Who made this for you — do you know the song that reminds them of home — do you know to play the radio as loud as you can and roll down the windows and smack your cheeks ten times in order to stay awake for the drive — do you know who sewed on this button — do you know the murmuring leg ache from standing all day a tree for whom — do you know who processed the letter you received today — fed it into a machine with paper cuts as wide as a river you could float in — do you know how long you can hold your urine until your 15-minute break — the roiling pressure in the

abdomen the tick-tap of the feet the hands — how much to tip the gas attendant in Jersey how the smell sticks behind both earlobes — the temperature when flipping a wok the oil burns the white-papered hat measuring salt at the brim — how your impatient face resembles a slowly rotting peach — worms in the snarl — do you know the name of your fishmonger the name of my uncle the times he has snuck in a call to say he will be late picking up his daughter fish scales glittered to his elbows like opera gloves — do you know cuticles peeling white like flecks of cod after washing dishes — do you know the smell of nail polish remover stinging bees in your nostrils — do you know the back — how the back curls how the back bridges how the back puckers and crunches — like packed snow no one else but you will shovel out —

       I look up how labor is used in a sentence — "the obvious labor" — "immigrants provided a source of cheap labor" — "negotiations between labor and management" — "wants the vote of labor in the elections" — "the flood destroyed the labor of years" — "industry needs labor for production" — anthropocene capitalism gentrification – what do these words mean – and to whom — helping my mother over the sink — I snip the ends of long beans 豆角 with kitchen shears – the ends rolling away — little green lizard tails – I cut away each word like a long bean — gentrificat — gentrif — gen — ge — g — glugging the g — down the drain —   If only lying on a beach — limbs loosened like an old garden hose — if only watching the movements of our stomachs — rising and falling like baby jellyfish — our thighs waxing and waning — in bristle-rough sand if only — reading a book the pages — wrinkled and curled like a snail shell — from falling asleep against our faces — if only devouring a cloud — full of no rain no metallic muscle if — only softness if only we —went off in the softness — into the downy relaxing abyss — what is this word — vacation — my grandmother asks me chili oil hitting the wok like delicious dying stars —   My grandmother said it was going to be long — going out the door always late for work — shirt inside out — said go on and bounce a howling baby (my mother/me/et al) – while skimming oxtail broth — the fat sheen of look how well we eat in this country —lest you forget it was worth it — lest you forget — the dilation of the cervix going the contractions going the grip the placenta the shit the vernix the garbled life going the soft flashlight eyes the milk the teeth the nails the hand on heart the soup coagulating on the stove — you must go — for what gleams in the dark turns to look at you — remember this — the work and the afterwork and the work of being perceived as not doing enough work though you are working well over enough — will this ever be enough — when is enough enough — the chorus now: not until the knots of fat — melt in this wok — not until you have nothing left but this suet — this smear of high heat lineage — gleaming in the gloaming — and it is yours and it is mine and it is your dream daughter's and it will last longer than you will ever believe — believe us —

AFTER PREPARING THE ALTAR, THE GHOSTS FEAST FEVERISHLY

How hard it is to sleep
in the middle of a life
—Audre Lorde

We wake in the middle of a life,   hungry.
We smear durian   along our mouths, sing soft
death a lullaby. Carcass breath, eros of licked fingers
and the finest perfume. What is love if not   rot?
We wear the fruit's hull as a spiked crown, grinning
in green armor.   Death to the grub, fat in his milky
shuffle! Death to the lawlessness   of dirt! Death
to mud and its false chocolate!   To the bloated sun
we want to slice open and yolk   all over
the village. We want a sun-drenched   slug feast,
an omelet loosening its folds like hot Jell-O. We want
the marbled fat of steak and all   its swirling pink
galaxies. We want the drool, the gnash, the pluck of
each corn kernel, raw and summer   swell.
Tears welling up   oil. Order up! Pickled
cucumbers piled like logs for a fire, like fat limbs we
pepper and succulent   in. Order up: Shrimp
chips curling in a porcelain bowl like subway seats.
Grapes peeled from bitter bark – almost translucent,
like eyes we would rather see. Little girl, what do you
leave, leaven   in your sight? Death to the open
eyes of the dying. Here,   there are so many open
eyes we can't close each one.   No, we did not say
the steamed eye of a fish. No eyelids fluttering like
no butterfly wings. No purple yam lips. We said eyes.
Still and resolute as a heartbreaker.   Does this break
your heart?   Look, we don't want
to be rude, but seconds, please. Want: globes of oranges
swallowed whole like a basketball or Mars or whatever
planet is the most delicious.   Slather Saturn!
Ferment Mercury!   Lap up its film of dust!
Seconds, thirds, fourths! Meat wool! A bouquet of

chicken feet! A garden of   melons, monstrous
in their bulge!   Prune back nothing. We purr
in this garden. We comb through berries and come out
so blue. Little girl,   lasso tofu, the rope
slicing its belly clean. Deep fry a cloud so it tastes like
bitter gourd or your father leaving—the exhaust of
his car, charred. Serenade a snake and slither its tongue
into yours and   bite. Love! What is love
if not knotted in garlic? Child, we move through graves
like eels, delicious   with our heads first, our mouths
agape. Our teeth: little needles to stitch a factory of
everything made in China.   You ask: Are you hungry?
Hunger eats through the air like ozone. You ask: What
does it mean to be rootless? Roots are good to use as
toothpicks. You: How can you wake in the middle of
a life? We shut and open our eyes like the sun shining
on tossed pennies in a forgotten well. Bald copper,
blood. Yu choy bolts   into roses down here.
While you were sleeping, we woke to the old leaves
of your backyard shed and ate that and one of your
lost flip-flops too. In a future life, we saw rats overtake
a supermarket with so much milk, we turned opaque.
We wake to something boiling. We wake to wash dirt
from lettuce, to blossom into your face. Aphids along
the lashes. Little girl, don't forget   to take care
of the chickens, squawking in their mess and stench.
Did our mouths buckle   at the sight
of you devouring slice   after slice of pizza and
the greasy box too? Does this frontier swoon for you?
It's time to wake up. Wake the tapeworm who loves
his home. Wake the ants,   let them do-si-do
a spoonful of peanut butter. Tell us, little girl, are you
hungry, awake,   astonished enough?

NOTES AND ACKNOWLEDGMENTS

Many thanks to the editors and readers of the following publications, in which versions of these poems first appeared:

POETRY, "Everything," "The Long Labors," and "After Preparing the Altar, the Ghosts Feast Feverishly"
Poetry Northwest, "An Altar"
AGNI, "Tenants"
The Massachusetts Review, "A Cosmology"
jubilat, from "When You Died"
Gulf Coast, "Unkindly Kind"
Burnside Review, from "The Frontier"
Redivider, "The Beet"
Figure 1, "What I Tell Myself after Waking Up with Fists"
Gramma, "Mad" and "The Egg"
The Adroit Journal, "What I Tell Myself before I Sleep" and "Lessons on Lessening"
Seedings, "The Cactus," and from "When You Died"
Bennington Review, from "When You Died"
Yemassee, from "When You Died"
DUSIE, from "When You Died"
The American Poetry Review, "I Put on My Fur Coat" (2016 Stanley Kunitz Memorial Prize)
Sink Review, "Notes for the Interior"
The Foundry, from "When You Died"
Underblong, from "When You Died"
COAST/no COAST, from "The Frontier"
Entropy, "Wrong June," from "When You Died," and "How to Not Be Afraid of Everything"
The Asian American Literary Review, from "When You Died"
The Volta, "Dream of the Lopsided Crown"
Lantern Review: "After He Travels through Ash, My Grandfather Speaks"
OmniVerse, "What Is Love if Not Rot"

"After Preparing the Altar, the Ghosts Feast Feverishly" (first published in *POETRY*) also appears in the anthology, *The World I Leave You: Asian American Poets on Faith and Spirit* (edited by Leah Silvieus and Lee Herrick) and on *Poetry Daily*. This poem was also reworked into a sculptural poem for a solo art exhibition at the Frye Art Museum in Seattle, along with "What Is Love if Not Rot" ("Jane Wong: After Preparing the Altar, the Ghosts Feast Feverishly," June-September 2019).

An excerpt of "When You Died" (first published in *The Foundry*) received a 2018 Pushcart Prize and appears in *The Pushcart Prize Anthology XLII,* edited by Bill Henderson.

"When You Died": From 1958 to 1962, the Great Leap Forward was a Maoist campaign that sought agricultural and industrial reform in the countryside. This campaign, also known as the Great Famine, resulted in an estimated 36 million deaths due to starvation. My grandfather survived the famine. Orphaned, he was adopted by an older man who also lost his family. My mother was born at the end of the Great Leap Forward and the start of the Cultural Revolution. This poem is for my missing family members and those who perished during the Great Leap Forward. With gratitude to Yang Jisheng's book *Tombstone* in particular.

I peel fruit for those I love. In writing this book, I am peeling heaps of apples, oranges, pears, mangoes, and longan for my mother, my little brother, my Pau Pau, my extended family, and my ancestors. May these seeds of sweetness kiss you, daily.

In roiling hot pot joy, an extra thank you to these dear writers who have supported this book with bright encouragement and nourishing friendship along the way: Michelle Peñaloza, Diana Khoi Nguyen, Anastacia-Renée, Naa Akua, Tessa Hulls, Eddie Kim, Nicholas Gulig, Dan Lau, Sally Wen Mao, Cathy Linh Che, Quenton Baker, Paul Hlava, Bill Carty, Catina Bacote, Brenda Miller, and Rick Barot. Many glistening dumpling hugs to Chen Chen, Kamilah Aisha Moon, and Aimee Nezhukumatathil for their heart-opening words about the book. Otters-holding-hands gratitude to Weston LeMay for making me coffee every damn day.

Mounds of gratitude to the brilliant and generous team at Alice James Books, especially Carey Salerno, Alyssa Neptune, Emily Marquis, and Julia Bouwsma. This book is a vulnerable one, and your faith in it blankets me. Thank you to Kimothy Wu, whose art simmers across the cover.

Grateful for the time, space, and support to eat snacks and dream these poems; thank you to Hedgebrook, Willapa Bay Artist in Residence Program, the Jentel Artist Residency Program, Sundress Academy of the Arts, the Sarabande Writing Residency at Blackacre, the Whiteley Center, Mineral School, and Western Washington University. Thank you to my visionary students who grow with me. My Kundiman community, thank you, and let's dance soon. Open Books and Elliott Bay Books, I love you. Especially grateful for the

James W. Ray Distinguished Artist Award from Artist Trust and the Frye Art Museum; the sheer fact that I was able to transform my poetry into an art exhibition was other-worldly. Extra thank you to David Strand, Amanda Donnan, and Shane Montgomery. I will never forget that moment when my entire family walked into the exhibit, altar-first, in glowing tears.

In the afterlife, cured pork belly and the sweetest oranges for my Gung Gung. Plump grapes and the warmest Dunkin Donuts coffee for my Ngin Ngin and my Yeh Yeh. I am here, your little bao bao, always.

RECENT TITLES FROM ALICE JAMES BOOKS

Brocken Spectre, Jacques J. Rancourt
No Ruined Stone, Shara McCallum
The Vault, Andrés Cerpa
White Campion, Donald Revell
Last Days, Tamiko Beyer
If This Is the Age We End Discovery, Rosebud Ben-Oni
Pretty Tripwire, Alessandra Lynch
Inheritance, Taylor Johnson
The Voice of Sheila Chandra, Kazim Ali
Arrow, Sumita Chakraborty
Country, Living, Ira Sadoff
Hot with the Bad Things, Lucia LoTempio
Witch, Philip Matthews
Neck of the Woods, Amy Woolard
Little Envelope of Earth Conditions, Cori A. Winrock
Aviva-No, Shimon Adaf, Translated by Yael Segalovitz
Half/Life: New & Selected Poems, Jeffrey Thomson
Odes to Lithium, Shira Erlichman
Here All Night, Jill McDonough
To the Wren: Collected & New Poems, Jane Mead
Angel Bones, Ilyse Kusnetz
Monsters I Have Been, Kenji C. Liu
Soft Science, Franny Choi
Bicycle in a Ransacked City: An Elegy, Andrés Cerpa
Anaphora, Kevin Goodan
Ghost, like a Place, Iain Haley Pollock
Isako Isako, Mia Ayumi Malhotra
Of Marriage, Nicole Cooley
The English Boat, Donald Revell
We, the Almighty Fires, Anna Rose Welch
DiVida, Monica A. Hand
pray me stay eager, Ellen Doré Watson

Alice James Books is committed to publishing books that matter. The press was founded in 1973 in Boston, Massachusetts as a cooperative, wherein authors performed the day-to-day undertakings of the press. This element remains present today, as authors who publish with the press are invited to collaborate closely in the publication process of their work. AJB remains committed to its founders' original feminist mission, while expanding upon the scope to include all voices and poets who might otherwise go unheard. In keeping with its efforts to build equity and increase inclusivity in publishing and the literary arts, AJB seeks out poets whose writing possesses the range, depth, and ability to cultivate empathy in our world and to dynamically push against silence. The press was named for Alice James, sister to William and Henry, whose extraordinary gift for writing went unrecognized during her lifetime.

Designed by Francine Kass

Printed by McNaughton & Gunn